To my brother, Obi, Ife, Chinaza
and their parents for their great support

JANETTA OTTER-BARRY BOOKS

First published in Great Britain in 2013 and in the USA in 2014 by
Frances Lincoln Children's Books, 4 Torriano Mews,
Torriano Avenue, London NW5 2RZ
www.franceslincoln.com

A catalogue record for this book is available from the British Library.

ISBN 978-1-84780-364-1

Set in Green

Printed in Shenzhen, Guangdong, China by CGC Offset Printing in May, 2013.

135798642

IFE'S
FIRST HAIRCUT

Ifeoma Onyefulu

F

FRANCES LINCOLN
CHILDREN'S BOOKS

This is Chinaza

and this is Chinaza's brother, Ife.

Chinaza loves playing with Ife.

But one day she says to Mama, "Ife's hair is too thick. He cries when I comb it."

Mama smiles. "Don't worry, my child," she says. "Your brother will have his first haircut very soon."

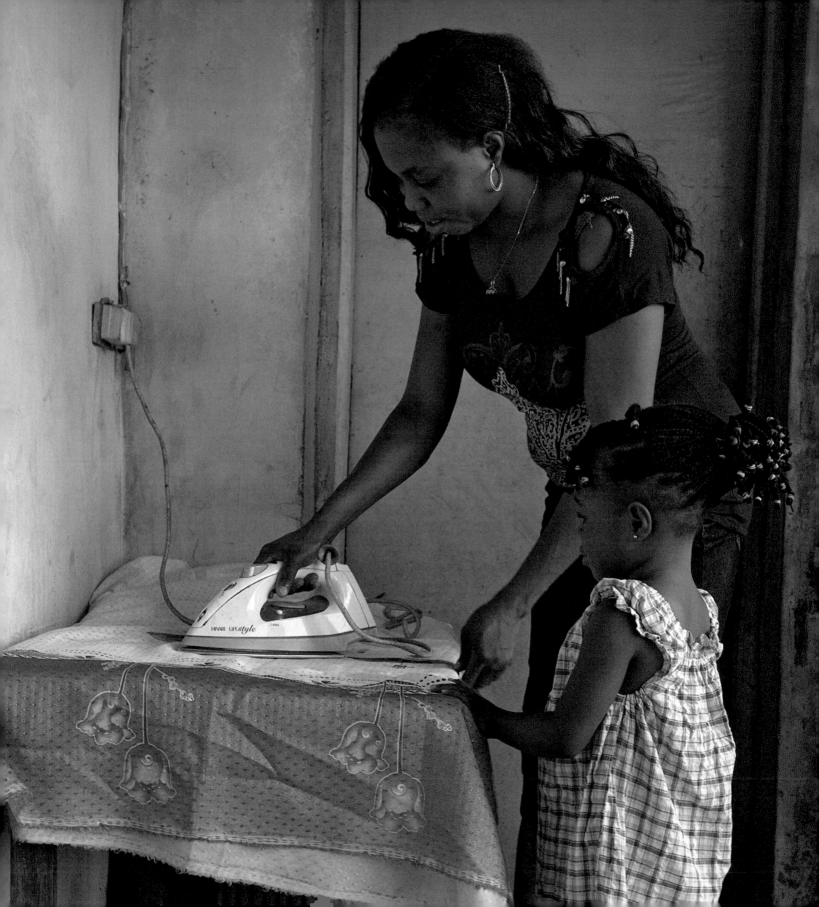

Chinaza is very excited.

"I want him to have a haircut right now, Mama!"

"Not now, child," says Mama.

"He'll have a haircut next week."

"Next week? That's a long time!" says Chinaza.

She goes to see Papa. "Don't worry, Chinaza," Papa smiles. "We'll have a party, too!"

"Why?" asks Chinaza.

"When a baby gets older, his hair changes, " says Papa. "To help his new hair grow better he has to have his hair cut. That's why it is special. So we are going to celebrate Ife's first haircut."

Next day Chinaza has another question
for Papa. "Did I have a haircut and a party
when I was a baby?" she asks.
Papa laughs. "Of course, my child.
Everyone has a little party when they have
their hair cut for the first time."

At last it is the big day! Mama and Papa
go to market to buy new clothes for Ife
and food for the party.

Later, Auntie Stella helps with the cooking. She is making rice, and will cook tomato sauce with beef, too.

Then Uncle Mike arrives
to cut Ife's hair. He shows Chinaza
a comb and a pair of scissors.
Chinaza is very excited.

Mama picks up Ife and sits him on her lap.
But Ife wants to run off and play,
so Uncle Mike will have to be quick.

First he cuts
the front.

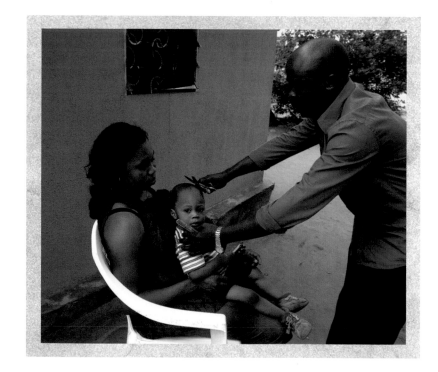

Then he cuts
one side, and
the other side...

and finally he cuts the back.

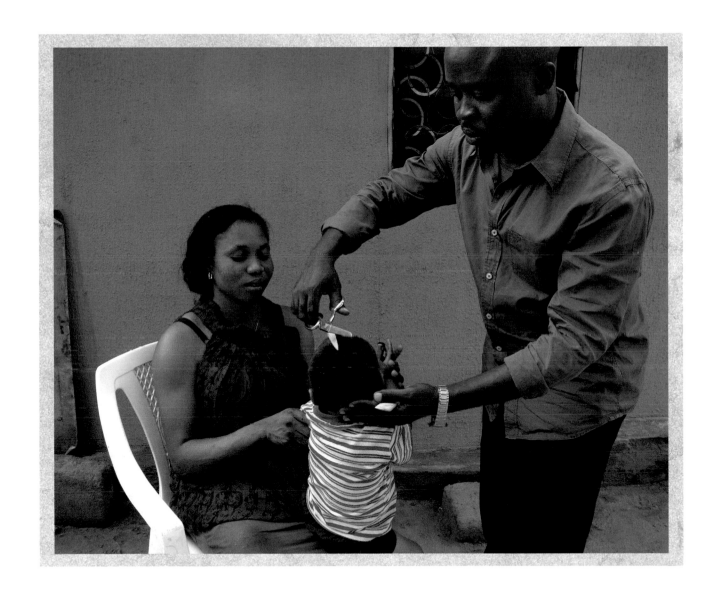

But will Uncle Mike finish in time?

At last!

Ife's hair isn't too thick

any more.

It looks great!

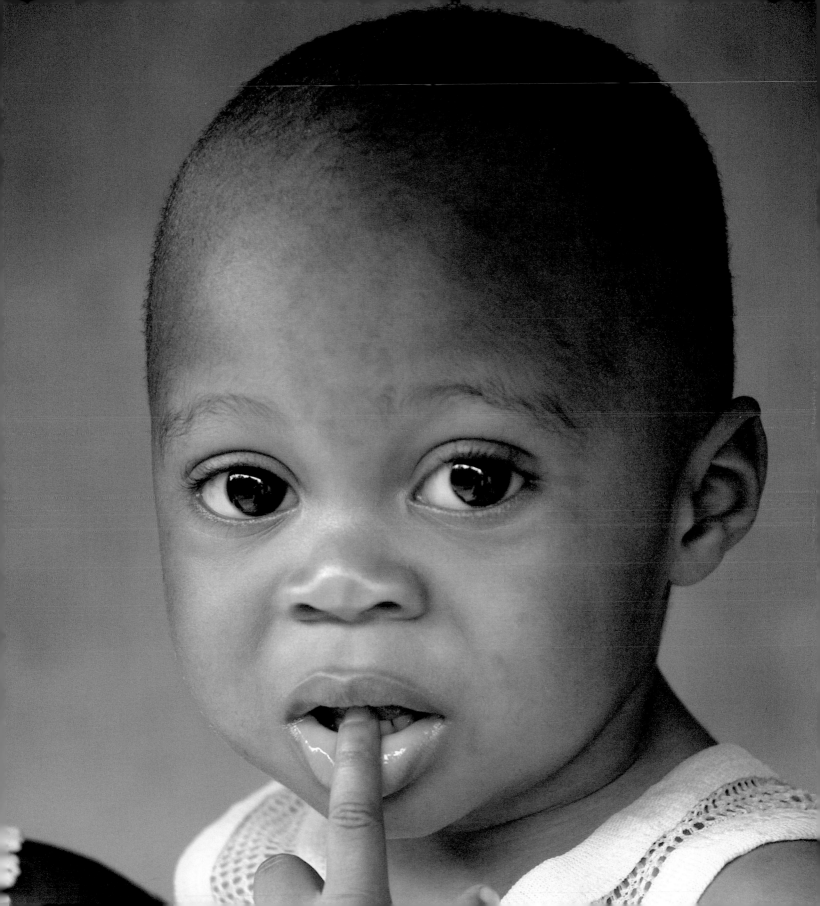

In the evening, friends
and relatives come
to Ife's party.

Here they are, eating delicious food,

singing and dancing.
It's a lovely party!

Now Chinaza is happy,
and her brother has had
his very first haircut.